LEGACIES

POLITICS AND GOVERNMENT

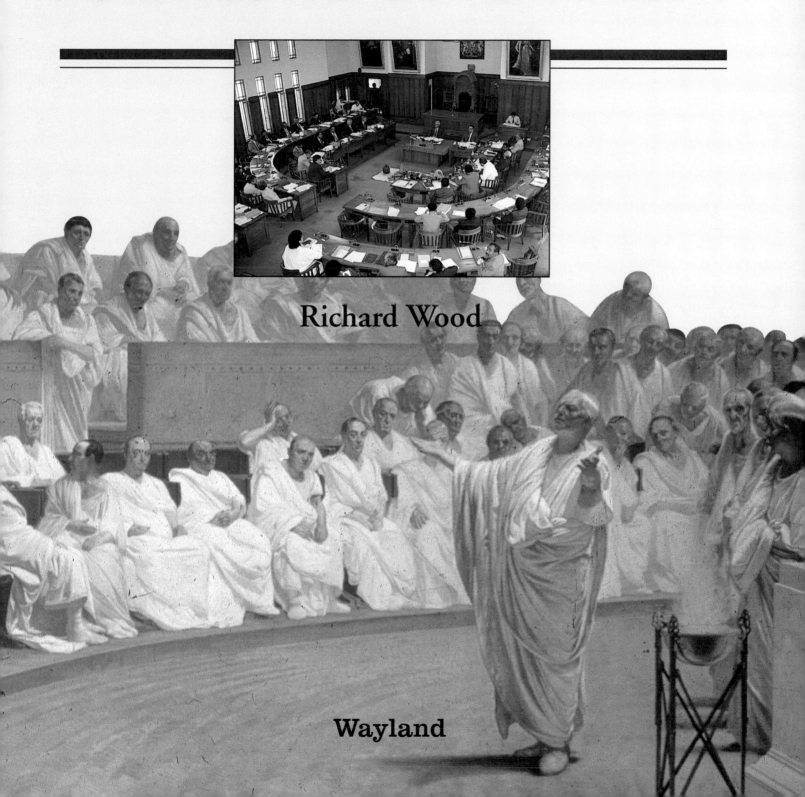

Richard Wood

Wayland

Legacies

Architecture
Costume and Clothes
Language and Writing
Politics and Government
Science and Technology
Sports and Entertainment

Cover pictures: A nineteenth-century painting of the ancient Roman Senate (main) and modern politicians meeting in a forum in Fiji Parliament House (inset).

Series and book editor: Polly Goodman
Researcher: Katherine Thomson
Series designer: Liz Miller
Book designer: Malcolm Walker

First published in 1995 by
Wayland (Publishers) Limited
61 Western Road, Hove
East Sussex BN3 1JD, England

British Library Cataloguing in Publication Data
   Wood, Richard
   Politics and Government. – (Legacies Series)
   I. Title II. Series
   320.09

ISBN 0 7502 1270 5

Typeset by Kudos Editorial and Design Services, England
Printed and bound in Italy by G. Canale & C.S.p.A., Turin

Contents

Legacies are things that are handed down from an ancestor or predecessor. The modern world has inherited many different legacies from ancient civilizations. This book explores the legacies of politics and government from the ancient world.

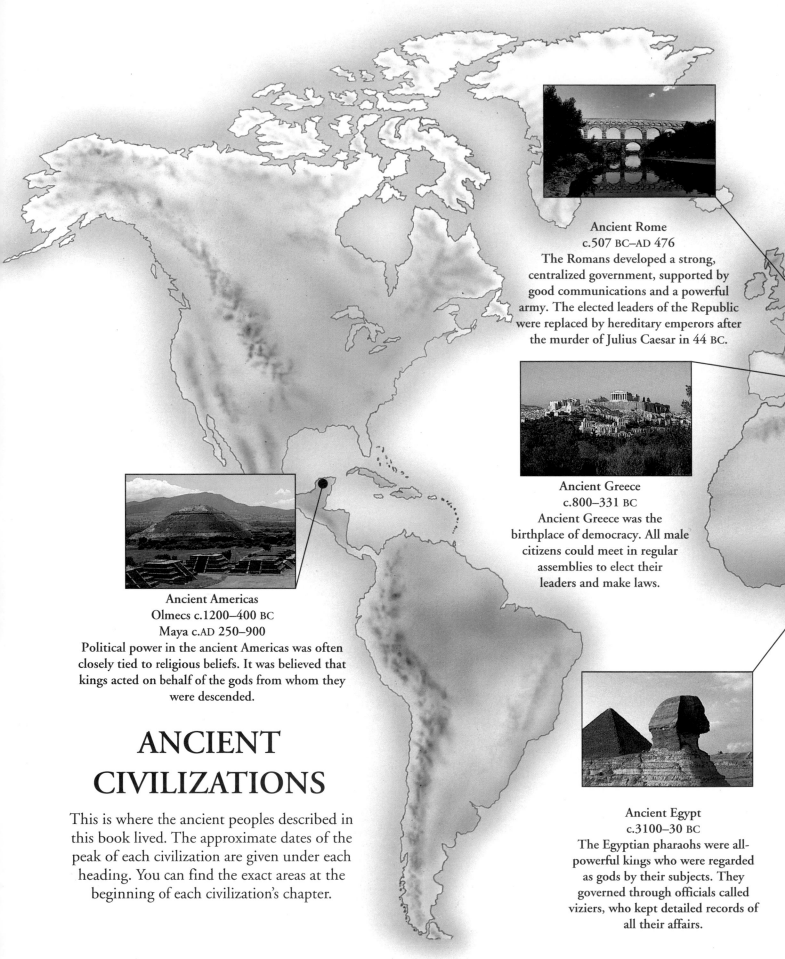

Ancient Rome
c.507 BC–AD 476
The Romans developed a strong, centralized government, supported by good communications and a powerful army. The elected leaders of the Republic were replaced by hereditary emperors after the murder of Julius Caesar in 44 BC.

Ancient Greece
c.800–331 BC
Ancient Greece was the birthplace of democracy. All male citizens could meet in regular assemblies to elect their leaders and make laws.

Ancient Americas
Olmecs c.1200–400 BC
Maya c.AD 250–900
Political power in the ancient Americas was often closely tied to religious beliefs. It was believed that kings acted on behalf of the gods from whom they were descended.

ANCIENT CIVILIZATIONS

This is where the ancient peoples described in this book lived. The approximate dates of the peak of each civilization are given under each heading. You can find the exact areas at the beginning of each civilization's chapter.

Ancient Egypt
c.3100–30 BC
The Egyptian pharaohs were all-powerful kings who were regarded as gods by their subjects. They governed through officials called viziers, who kept detailed records of all their affairs.

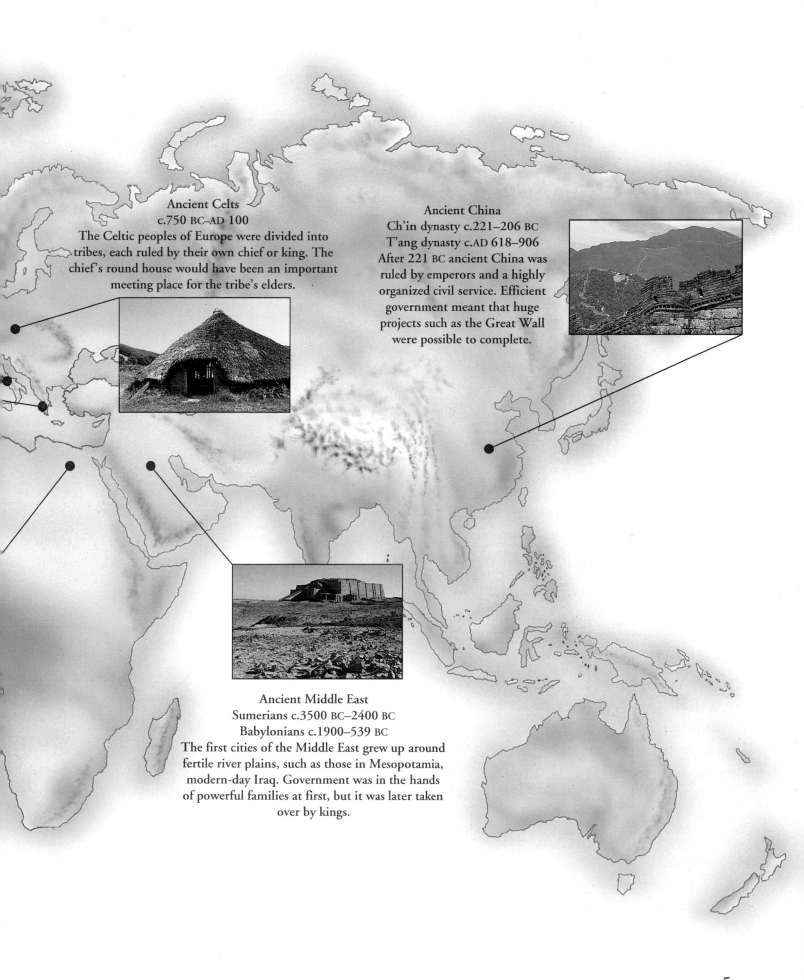

Ancient Celts
c.750 BC–AD 100
The Celtic peoples of Europe were divided into tribes, each ruled by their own chief or king. The chief's round house would have been an important meeting place for the tribe's elders.

Ancient China
Ch'in dynasty c.221–206 BC
T'ang dynasty c.AD 618–906
After 221 BC ancient China was ruled by emperors and a highly organized civil service. Efficient government meant that huge projects such as the Great Wall were possible to complete.

Ancient Middle East
Sumerians c.3500 BC–2400 BC
Babylonians c.1900–539 BC
The first cities of the Middle East grew up around fertile river plains, such as those in Mesopotamia, modern-day Iraq. Government was in the hands of powerful families at first, but it was later taken over by kings.

chapter one

POLITICS AND GOVERNMENT: MODERN AND ANCIENT

▼ *A nineteenth-century painting of ancient Roman government. During the Roman Republic, laws were passed by the Senate, a group of senators who met regularly to discuss political affairs. The layout of this room is very similar to modern parliament meeting rooms.*

The organization of our modern lives is a very complicated affair. Most of us live in communities that need detailed rules to keep them running smoothly. There are decisions to make, laws to enforce, public works to perform, armies to direct – and taxes to raise to pay for them. These are just some of the concerns of politics and government, which affect almost every aspect of our lives in some way.

Without effective government, there would be no schools or hospitals, nobody to get rid of rubbish or guarantee fresh water supplies to our homes, and nobody to protect us against crime or enemy attacks. Government is all about making sure that a country is run properly. Politics involves all the arguments about how this should be done.

Politics and government have existed, in one form or another, since the earliest times. The first people lived in family groups, or perhaps in small tribes or villages where everyone knew each other. It was easy for them to agree rules and to share jobs between them in a friendly fashion. But even then, there must have been arguments which needed to be sorted out. From the start, some people exercised more power than others. Maybe they were stronger, wiser or richer than others, or just more cunning or cruel so that others feared and obeyed them.

As soon as people began to live in larger communities, such as the first cities of the Middle East, more complicated arrangements were needed. It was in those early cities, over 5,000 years ago, that politics and government as we understand them today began. It is no accident that our word 'politics' comes from the ancient Greek word *polis*, which means city.

▲ *Modern politicians often meet in special parliament buildings, like this one in Fiji. The layout of the room enables many people to discuss things without leaving their seats. Debates are controlled from the raised chair at the far end.*

Ancient claim
Modern governments sometimes use ancient ideas. A 1990s Russian coin shows a two-headed eagle, the badge of ancient Rome. A century ago, the Russian rulers were called 'Czars' (Caesars) and claimed to be the successors of the Roman emperors.

More than 200 years ago, the writer Edmund Burke said that politics was 'the art of the possible'. Long before his time, the rulers of the ancient world had discovered the same thing. They found that personal strength and military power are never enough to keep a ruler in power for long. Even the harshest Roman emperors had to keep their own soldiers happy to avoid being assassinated. Like every modern politician, ancient rulers had to listen to other points of view and be prepared to compromise. Such debates are the basis of politics.

There are many different kinds of government. Monarchy (rule by a king or queen), tyranny (rule by a dictator who has seized power for him or herself), oligarchy or aristocracy (rule by a few rich or well-born people) and democracy (rule by the people themselves or their representatives) were all invented in ancient times. They are still used all over the world today.

Any community needs people to organize its activities and make decisions on behalf of the whole people. In the past, this role was usually taken by men, and most ancient societies were dominated by

◄ *This giant statue of Pharaoh Rameses II, which inspired the poet Shelley, was carved in about 1280 BC. It still stands today at Luxor in Egypt.*

men. There were exceptions, however. In ancient Mesopotamia, what is now called Iraq, women had the right to own land and property, conduct trade and even become judges. There were sometimes powerful women, such as the Egyptian queens Hatshepsut and Cleopatra, and the Celtic queen Boudicca. However, most women took little part in politics or government. Sadly, this is still true in many countries today. Even in the West, there are fewer women politicians than men, and many countries, such as Saudi Arabia, still deny women any real political rights.

Today, most of us do not meet our political leaders face to face very often, although they sometimes visit schools, hospitals and shopping centres, especially at election times. Their faces and opinions, however, are well known to us thanks to newspapers, radio and television. All politicians need opportunities to persuade people to support them. In ancient times, societies were quite small, so it was easy for many people to hear their leaders speaking in person. In the modern world, the most successful politicians are often those who perform best on (or have most control over) the mass media.

Dangers of power
The most powerful politicians are often the most hated. There were forty-six plots to kill Adolf Hitler, the dictator of Germany between 1934–45. One, in 1944, almost succeeded when a bomb exploded close to him. The plotters were hanged and Hitler sent the bills for the cost of their executions to their wives.

► People in politics have always led very public lives. Today they are often surrounded by news reporters and photographers. Here, Jeremy Hanley faces the press following his appointment as Chairman of the British Conservative Party, in July 1994.

chapter two

ANCIENT MIDDLE EAST

In primitive societies, most people must hunt, gather and farm for the food they need. However, ancient Mesopotamia (modern-day Iraq), like many richer countries today, had fertile, well-watered soil and could grow abundant food. Only a few people actually needed to work the land to feed the whole population. This left the rest free to become labourers, merchants, craftspeople, artists and officials, who came together to form cities.

The city of Uruk, called Warka today, was the first, and for a long time, the most powerful city. It began in about 3500 BC, and had about 50,000 inhabitants. At first, a Council of Elders ruled Uruk. They were the heads of the main families there. Even today, rich or noble families sometimes control towns and villages, a form of government known as aristocracy. The Uruk elders were sometimes priests, too. Religion was very important to the ancient Mesopotamians. People obeyed the elders partly because they believed that they ruled on behalf of their gods. Some modern rulers, especially in Islamic countries,

▼ *Stepped temples, called ziggurats, once towered over the cities of ancient Mesopotamia. They reminded people of the power of their gods, and of the kings who ruled on their behalf. This ziggurat still stands at Ur, in Iraq.*

combine religious authority with political power in a similar way. Even in Christian countries, politicians cannot afford to ignore the views of church leaders without risking unpopularity and perhaps defeat.

By about 2800 BC, there were about a dozen other cities in Mesopotamia. There were disputes between them, and sometimes they fought each other. In a time of war, orders must be given quickly. The elders of Uruk could not meet and make decisions fast enough, so they chose a 'lugal' (which means 'big man') to lead the city in war.

As wars became more frequent, the lugal's power grew. Before long, the lugal controlled the daily life of the city in peace as well as war, and even appointed his sons as his successors. The war leaders had become kings. For a time these kings of the different cities of Mesopotamia seemed to be almost permanently in conflict with each other. Eventually, in about 2500 BC, King Lugalzagessi of Uma conquered Uruk and about fifty smaller cities and for a time he became 'King of the whole land of Sumer'.

▲ **Writing**
Effective government of large populations, in ancient as well as modern times, would not have been possible without written records. Writing was invented in Mesopotamia in about 3500 BC, and scribes, who were trained in temple schools, became the first administrators. King Hammurabi of Babylon gave written instructions to his officials to tell them how to do their work.

Lugalzagessi's empire did not last long and in 2370 BC, the region of Sumer was conquered by King Sargon of Akkad. In time, his empire collapsed too, and power was seized by Ur (2112–2006 BC). All these men were great warriors. It was their military strength which gave them political power. In the modern world too, the most powerful countries and leaders are usually those with the strongest armies.

▲ When the dictators Francisco Franco and Benito Mussolini met in 1941, they both wore military uniforms. Both men depended on their armies for power.

The twentieth century has many examples of rulers who have gained power due to war. Some, like British Prime Minister Winston Churchill and French President Charles de Gaulle during the Second World War, have used their powers well. Others, like the military dictators Benito Mussolini of Italy or Francisco Franco of Spain, found that war provided an opportunity for them to take complete control of their countries. Some modern rulers, like Saddam Hussein in Iraq, have even started wars deliberately as a means of increasing their own power.

► The Mesopotamians believed that their gods were directly involved in government. This impression of a 4,000-year-old seal from Ur (modern-day Iraq) shows the goddess Ishtar presenting a new city governor to the king. Modern officials often still swear 'by Almighty God' to work honestly and faithfully on behalf of their governments.

By about 2500 BC, the kings of Mesopotamia seemed to be all-powerful in their cities. 'The king's word is right; his utterance, like that of a god, cannot be changed,' they said. But of course, no one person could personally control all the activities of such a large number of people. As in a modern state, there were many organizations, each looking after a different government job.

One of these organizations was the temple, which was made up of priests and temple officials. The temple was a powerful religious organization, which collected offerings for the gods who protected the city. It was also economically powerful, since it owned land and controlled the peasants who worked on it. At Lagash, temple officials employed 1,200 people, including blacksmiths, clothworkers, millers, bakers and cooks. Their builders, artists and sculptors helped to make the city powerful as well as beautiful. The temple also provided a sort of social service, by feeding the poor and looking after the sick. In times of catastrophes, such as flood or drought, it issued food rations from the temple granaries to help the whole community through. Modern governments, too, need to make sure that there is enough food to feed their populations.

A king's claim
'I provided unfailing water for the lands . . . I gathered the scattered people and provided them with pasture . . . I settled them in peaceful dwellings . . . I made justice in the land to destroy the wicked and evil-doer, that the strong may not harm the weak.'
(King Hammurabi of Babylon, 1792–59 BC)

▲ *Assyrian cooks prepare food in about 860 BC. Making sure there is enough food is one of the most basic responsibilities of all governments.*

▼ *John F. Kennedy was President of the USA from 1961–63, after being elected by a vast majority. However, even the most popular leaders have enemies, and Kennedy was shot while driving through Dallas. The circumstances of his death are still not fully explained.*

Craftspeople formed another large group in Mesopotamian cities, a sort of professional middle class. They were organized into units named after animals (as in the Scout movement today), each with its own responsibilities. The king could call on these units to help, for example, with harvesting, or with a crisis such as a broken dam. In times of war, the units were sent off to fight, each under the command of its own leader.

Most modern politicians come to power promising to help people and prevent injustice. Unfortunately, they sometimes forget their promises once they are elected! King Urukagina of Lagash (about 2600 BC) was one ancient ruler who really did try to improve people's lives. Urukagina's path to power was not blameless – he assassinated the previous king. But once he was in charge, he 'established the freedom' of his subjects. Some officials, like those who were in charge of supplying water for the fields, had become very rich by taxing the poor until they were almost starving. Urukagina expelled the tax gatherers and made sure that everybody had enough to eat. Not surprisingly, he was unpopular with the rich. After only ten years, he was overthrown. In modern times, too, leaders who set out to help ordinary people sometimes arouse strong hostility from others. American President John F. Kennedy faced much opposition when he tried to improve living conditions for black Americans during the early 1960s.

For any society to run smoothly, people need to understand and obey rules. King Hammurabi of Babylon (1792–59 BC) was one of the first rulers to establish a detailed code of laws for all to obey. His laws were inscribed on a great stone, called a stele, and set up for everyone to see. He also issued written instructions to his officials, telling them how they should work and handle state matters. Hammurabi's laws covered everything from murder to marriage and from trade to the rights of slaves and the wages of workers. There were law courts to enforce the rules, fixed punishments for offenders, and the right of appeal to the king if people were unfairly treated. The back of the stone on which the laws were written showed a picture of the Mesopotamian god Utu, god of the sun and justice. The god's figure reminded people that Hammurabi had made the laws on behalf of the god. Indeed, Hammurabi claimed that the god had dictated them to him in person.

▲ This stele, or stone pillar, is inscribed with the 200 laws of King Hammurabi of Babylon. At the top stands a figure of Uti, the Sumerian god of justice, presenting the laws to Hammurabi.

Ancient fines
'If a man bites the nose of another man and severs it, he shall pay one mina of silver; an eye, one mina; a tooth, half a mina; an ear, half a mina; a hit on the jaw, he shall pay ten shekels of silver.'
This law is one of many found on two ancient Mesopotamian clay tablets. The tablets, which date back to about 1900 BC, were found in Iraq in 1947. It shows that Babylonians living nearly 4,000 years ago believed in fair justice rather than revenge.

chapter three

ANCIENT EGYPT

In recent times, some leaders have been almost worshipped by their followers. Kim Il-Sung, the 'Great Leader' of North Korea for forty-six years, was a modern dictator who did little good for his people. Yet he encouraged such adoration from his people that 50,000 statues of him were erected. When he died in 1994, millions of people took to the streets, hysterically crying with grief. Kim Il-Sung was almost like a god to his followers. The ancient Egyptians believed that their kings, called pharaohs, really were gods. This made them even more powerful in the eyes of their people than the Mesopotamian kings, who merely acted on behalf of the gods.

This close connection between rulers and gods is another political legacy of ancient times. In the Islamic world, the rulers of Iran govern on behalf of Allah (God), imposing the Islamic Law of the Qur'an, their holy book. British coins state that the Queen rules 'Dei Gratia' ('by the grace of God') and is

▼ *The great stone pyramids of Egypt were built about 2600 BC. They were intended to preserve the divine bodies of the pharaohs for ever.*

'Fidei Defensor' ('Defender of the Faith'). This claim was in the news recently. The Prince of Wales, who will probably be the next British king, is unhappy with the title he is to take on. He would rather be called 'defender of faiths', because members of many different religions now live in Britain.

The ancient Egyptians believed that when a new pharaoh came to the throne, the spirit of the hawk-headed god Horus entered him. He became the god on earth. He alone could worship the other gods on behalf of the people. His power was total in all areas of government – making laws, directing public works, waging wars and imposing taxes.

Because of their divine descent, the blood of the Egyptian pharaohs had to be kept 'pure'. To ensure this, many pharaohs married their sisters. Amenophis III (1417–1374 BC) even married his own daughter Sitamun, as well as his main wife, Tiye. His son Akhenaten (1379–62 BC) in turn had children by two of his own daughters.

▲ **A modern leader's pyramid** *When Lenin (the leader of the 1917 Russian Revolution) died, his body was embalmed like an Egyptian pharaoh. It can still be seen in a pyramid-shaped tomb in Moscow's Red Square.*

Unlike the Mesopotamian kings, the Egyptian pharaohs did not make special efforts to rule for the benefit of the people. However, the god-like powers they were believed to hold were supposed to bring prosperity to their people. In theory, all the people were the pharaoh's slaves and they lived only in order to serve him. Politics, in the modern sense of debate and policy-making, hardly existed in ancient Egypt. Discussion of public affairs was forbidden and people had no political rights. There are still some countries today – China, Iraq and North Korea, for example – where people are forbidden to speak against their governments. Powerful armies or secret police forces are needed to enforce their authority. But in ancient Egypt, most people accepted this situation without question, because their pharaoh was believed to hold the power to make their crops grow. There was no need for the pharaohs to employ secret police because people willingly accepted their power.

To help him rule, the pharaoh employed officials, or viziers, to manage such things as taxes, law, trade and farming. These people were often related to each other and to the pharaoh, who knew he could trust them. They were thoroughly trained at the royal palace and became

◀ *Women normally played no direct part in the government of Egypt. But when Pharaoh Tutmosis died in 1479 BC, his widow Hatshepsut (left) pushed her stepson aside and ruled as queen for twenty years. Her terraced temple at Deir el-Bahri is one of the grandest surviving monuments of this period of Egyptian history. After Hatshepsut died, her successor Tutmosis III tried to erase her memory by cutting her figure off all the statues.*

the world's first civil service. Thanks to their efficient organization, and to the unquestioned authority of pharaohs, the Egyptians were able to carry out vast drainage schemes and public building programmes. Some of these buildings, like the Pyramids at Giza, have survived to this day.

Perhaps the most famous vizier of all was not even a native Egyptian, but the Israelite Joseph, whose story is told in the Bible. One passage describes a ceremony often illustrated in Egyptian tomb paintings: 'Pharaoh said to Joseph, "I give you authority over the whole land of Egypt." He took off his ring and put it on Joseph's finger. He had him dressed in fine linen and hung a gold chain round his neck. He mounted him on his chariot and men cried out "make way" before him.' Occasions like this are very important in the political life of modern as well as ancient societies. Most modern-day politicians receive power at formal oath-taking or swearing-in ceremonies similar to those which must have taken place in ancient times.

◀ *Bill Clinton takes the oath of office as President of the USA, in January 1993. Such ceremonies are a modern version of an ancient practice.*

chapter four

ANCIENT GREECE

Most people in the modern Western world live in democratic countries. This means that all adults have the chance to vote in elections to choose the people who will govern the country. In theory, at least, this system ensures that the government represents the views of most of the people.

Our word 'democracy' comes from the ancient Greek word *demos*, meaning 'the people'. Democracy means 'rule by the people'. It is hardly surprising that we are still using an ancient Greek term, since it was the Greeks of Athens who invented democracy, 2,500 years ago. Of all the political legacies of ancient times, democracy is the most powerful today.

▼ *Some of the most beautiful temples of Athens, which stand on a hill called the Acropolis, were built on the orders of Pericles. They are a permanent monument to the success of the democratic reforms which he introduced.*

The landscape of Greece may explain why democracy first emerged there. Greece is a small country with steep mountains and a jagged coastline. From early times, small city states developed. Although their peoples spoke the same language, they were cut off from each other.

This was no place for a single, all-powerful king to rule, as in Egypt.

Recent years have seen many great political upheavals which have affected the lives of millions. In Eastern Europe, the former Soviet Union, South Africa and elsewhere, people have had a real say in choosing their governments for the first time. An ancient Mesopotamian or Egyptian would probably be amazed by such events. But an ancient Greek would feel quite at home. The Greeks knew, as many people are discovering today, that democracy is not something that arrives overnight. It usually comes only after a long and bitter struggle.

In Greece, this struggle lasted for 150 years. During this time, power passed gradually from the old aristocracy into the hands of ordinary male citizens. Greek women never got to vote – but even in the modern world they have had to wait until the twentieth century for this. This does not mean that women were not concerned about politics. The comic plays of the ancient Greek writer Aristophanes suggest that women often had considerable influence over their husbands.

▲ *Voting in the South African elections of April, 1994. For the first time, black people were allowed to vote in national elections, and so have a say in choosing their own government.*

Elections
Elections involve choosing from a list of candidates. Today, most political candidates stand as members of political parties such as the Republicans or Democrats in the USA, or the Labour, Liberal Democrat or Conservative Parties in Britain. Thanks to the press and television, their ideas and opinions are usually well known.

The Greek state, known as a 'polis' (as in 'politics'), consisted of a walled city and its surrounding countryside. Life centred on the city market, temples, meeting places and law courts. Poor people, women, children, slaves and foreigners were not counted as citizens, so they had no say in politics or government at all. Today, children still have no vote. Nor do women in many Middle Eastern countries. Some states, like Germany, do not allow foreign 'guest workers' to vote, and in Britain and the USA, poor people have only been allowed to vote for just over a century, and women for even less.

Athens, where democracy began, once had kings. By about 700 BC, government was generally in the hands of the leaders of the richest families, called 'archons'. This was a form of government called an oligarchy. The archons met in the Areopagus Council (a sort of government cabinet) and made laws for everyone else to follow. Their laws were not always popular, however, since they often favoured the rich over the poor. In 624 BC, the archon Draco published a set of laws which were so strict that we still use the word 'draconian' to describe a very severe rule. As the Roman writer Plutarch wrote: 'Under the Draconian code, almost any kind of offence was liable to the death penalty . . . and those who stole fruit suffered the same punishment as those who committed murder. Draco's code was written not in ink, but in blood.'

However, things started to change. More people learned to read, and they began to question the laws of the archons. (Education has been very important in the spread of modern democracy, too.) Middle-class Athenians became more important in the army,

Publishing the news
Athenian laws were written on both sides of strong wooden slabs called 'axones'. These rotated so that they did not take up too much space but could easily be read. They were set up in the market-place, where many people could see and read them. Today, public notices, newspaper headlines and television news bulletins serve a similar purpose. Being able to read was as important to the rise of democracy in ancient Greece as it is in politics today.

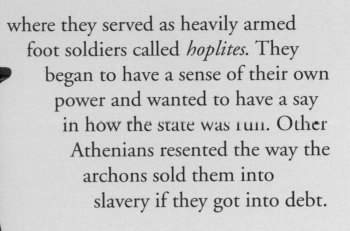

where they served as heavily armed foot soldiers called *hoplites*. They began to have a sense of their own power and wanted to have a say in how the state was run. Other Athenians resented the way the archons sold them into slavery if they got into debt.

◄ *This Greek jug from Athens shows foot soldiers, known as* hoplites. *Hoplites were heavily armed, strictly disciplined and trained to fight in close ranks called* phalanxes. *They were mostly small farmers or landowners who could afford to buy their own armour and weapons. The leaders of the ancient Greek cities relied on these men for success in battle. In return they allowed the men to become citizens, with the right to vote in the Assembly.*

23

The champion of the discontented Athenians was called Solon. He was appointed as a special magistrate in 594 BC to prevent a civil war between the rich and the poor. Solon was a poet whose songs about right and wrong, wealth and poverty, were popular with all classes. In some ways, the modern Czech leader, Vaclav Havel, is a present-day Solon – the popularity of his plays about the wrongs of the old Communist government helped him to be chosen as Czechoslovakia's president when change came in 1989.

▼ *Solon used his gifts as a poet and public speaker to persuade the rich landowners to give some power to the people without land. His ideas saved Athens from a civil war between rich and poor.*

In ancient Greece, Solon's reforms were very popular. He released the farmers from debt and freed those who had been enslaved for getting into debt. He restricted the powers of the Areopagus Council, and allowed poorer citizens to join others in a special meeting called the Assembly to discuss affairs. Solon did not establish democracy, and his reforms did not free everyone in ancient Greece – thousands of slaves stayed in captivity. However, for the first time he allowed ordinary people some political rights. The idea that the people are the rulers of the state, not its servants, was born. This vital principle has been the basis of every democratic government to this day.

Solon's boast
'The laws I have written are for noblemen and commoner alike. They give straight justice to everybody.'

For Solon and other Greek political leaders, oratory (public speaking) was one of their most vital skills. Ancient Greek politicians were called orators because they used their speeches to influence voters in the Assembly. A person's ability in public speaking can still affect his or her success, not only in politics, but in many other areas of life where it is necessary to persuade others. Politics are still conducted in most countries of the world by public argument and debate. Whether it is the United Nations, the European Parliament or some smaller national assembly, their methods are a direct legacy of ancient Greek times.

◄ Oracles
Religion did not play such an important part in the politics of Greece as it had in Mesopotamia and Egypt. Even so, no important decision was made without consulting the gods for an oracle, or opinion about what would happen. The most famous oracle was at Delphi (left). Here the god Apollo spoke through an old peasant woman, called the Pythia. She went into a trance to give utterances. Since oracles could always be understood in more than one way, they could never be proved wrong.

A whiff of scandal
The private lives of politicians often interest and concern ordinary voters, as President Bill Clinton of the USA and David Mellor in Britain both found out. Both politicians became the centre of media attention over their personal lives. This was true in ancient times, too. Pericles nearly lost power when he fell in love with a beautiful woman called Aspasia. People resented her influence over him, particularly because she was a foreigner.

▼ *This piece of pottery bears the name of Aristeides, who was ostracized from Athens in 482 BC when he opposed spending money on new war ships.*

If one date marks the 'invention' of democracy, it is 505 BC. This was when Cleisthenes, the leader of one of the Greek tribes, introduced further reforms which gave the people's Assembly more power in government.

The Assembly was like a modern parliament. But instead of its members being elected as representatives, every adult male citizen could attend, speak and vote. In this respect, the Greek system was more democratic than in many countries today. The Assembly met on forty days each year. Sometimes as many as 5,000 men turned up to take part.

Of course, it was impossible for all of them to have a say. Cleisthenes therefore introduced a new council of 500 men, called the 'Boule', who did most of the day-to-day work on behalf of the whole Assembly. The archons still met in the Areopagus, but now they had much less power.

To stop any one man becoming too powerful in the assembly, Cleisthenes introduced the law of ostracism. Once a year, people could name anyone they wanted to expel from Athens. They wrote their names on bits of broken pottery called 'ostraca'. Anyone whose name appeared on more than 6,000 ostraca was sent away (ostracized) for ten years.

Perhaps the greatest Athenian politician of all was Pericles, who led Athens for thirty years until his death in 429 BC. Pericles wanted power for Athens. He used the navy to conquer other lands, founded an empire and made the city richer than ever before. Pericles spent this wealth on building the great temples that we can still see today on the Acropolis in Athens (see pages 20–21).

Above all, however, Pericles fought for the rights of ordinary people against the rich. When he found that poorer men could not afford to leave their jobs to attend the assembly, he introduced pay so that no one should be excluded. He finally ended the influence of the rich archons by closing the Areopagus. Naturally, the nobles were furious. They murdered Pericles' friend Ephialtes, but did not dare to touch Pericles because he was so loved by the people. For a time, those people of Athens who were privileged enough to be called citizens (only a seventh of its population) enjoyed the most complete democracy that the world has ever seen. The other six-sevenths, either women, slaves, or those who could not prove that both their parents were Athenian, enjoyed no democracy at all.

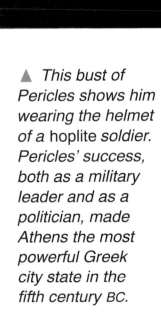

▲ *This bust of Pericles shows him wearing the helmet of a* hoplite *soldier. Pericles' success, both as a military leader and as a politician, made Athens the most powerful Greek city state in the fifth century BC.*

Champions of equality
'Power is in the hands of the whole people and everyone is equal before the law.' – Pericles (died 429 BC)

'There shall no longer be any doubt that all men are created free and equal.' – Abraham Lincoln (1809–65), President of the USA.

27

chapter five

ANCIENT
ROME

Census

After 443 BC, two officials, called 'censors', were appointed to register all Roman citizens every five years. People's names, ages and wealth were recorded to make it easier to tax them and enrol them for army service. Later, Roman censors became responsible for the morals of the people. Most modern governments still conduct censuses, and use 'censorship' to prevent the spread of harmful ideas or offensive pictures.

THE REPUBLIC

Look at how most countries are governed today, and you will find power shared among different groups of people. There is often a president in control of power, although some countries, like Britain and Sweden, still have kings or queens. Despite holding great power, the president cannot act alone. To make laws or raise taxes, the president needs the support of both an upper and a lower assembly. In the USA, these are the Senate and House of Representatives, in Britain they are the Houses of Lords and Commons.

Though each level of government has its own responsibilities, the checks and balances between them are a guarantee of freedom. This is a legacy from the Romans, who invented this system in the fifth century BC.

The Roman Republic lasted for 500 years until it was destroyed by civil war in 49 BC. Rome once had kings, but in about 500 BC, they were overthrown by wealthy families who established a republic instead. From then on, government was mainly in the hands of rich nobles. As in Athens, a class struggle developed between these nobles and the poor, who demanded a say in affairs. Eventually, after the first-recorded workers' strike, the nobles gave way. In about 471 BC, they gave the poor their own assembly and ten elected officials, called 'tribunes', to look after their interests.

The aristocrats in the Senate still did most of the decision-making. But the tribunes could veto (refuse to accept) the Senate's decisions if they went against the interests of ordinary citizens. The purpose of elected representatives in many countries today is similar. Laws are proposed, but the people's representatives must agree before any new laws become official.

The American constitution, upon which the American government is based, is a direct legacy from the ancient Roman Republic. Thomas Jefferson and the founding fathers of the constitution had all studied ancient history. They believed that they were recreating the Roman Republic when they drew up the American constitution. They copied the Roman balance of power and even named one of their bodies the 'Senate'.

Fasces
'Fasces' were rods and axes carried in front of Roman magistrates as a sign of their power to flog and execute criminals. The twentieth-century Italian dictator Mussolini used the fasces sign as a symbol of his power. His followers became known as Fascists.

▼ The forum, or market place, of ancient Rome as it appears today. Generations of Roman citizens must have met here to gossip about the great leaders and political events of the day.

The top Roman officials or magistrates were all chosen from the richest families. They held office for one year and had clear responsibilities – for taxes, roads, as town governors or judges, for example. Only the Censors held office for five years, but then they could not be reappointed. All the magistrates were led by two Consuls who acted almost like elected kings. Together, the magistrates acted like modern government ministers.

Under the magistrates came the Senate. This was a permanent council with almost 600 members, who controlled the money and supervised the law courts. The Senate was made up of former magistrates. They were not elected and held office for life, like members of the British House of Lords.

The people's assembly, or Comitia, consisted of representatives of all the adult males, chosen by their tribes. They chose the magistrates and passed or rejected the laws which the Senate proposed. As the Roman politician Cicero wrote, this system gave 'authority to the Senate but power to the people'. The ordinary people might not have agreed.

Few poor peasants could ever go to Rome to vote. They had no trained leaders or political parties. They were not allowed to debate issues but merely to vote 'yes' or 'no' – and were easily bribed to support whatever the

▼ *Marcus Tullius Cicero, 106–43 BC. Cicero was one of the greatest orators and writers of ancient Rome. He became a Consul, but was later put to death for his defence of the Republic after Caesar's death.*

◄ **Secret ballots**

◄ **Secret ballots**
Today, votes are cast in secret. This prevents rich or powerful people from influencing the vote by bribing or threatening voters. These are the Russian elections of April, 1993. In most countries, voters are given ballot papers with the names of the candidates listed on them. The voters secretly mark the names of the candidates they wish to vote for, then place the folded paper in a ballot box. Secret voting was introduced in the late Roman Republic. Citizens had to walk along a narrow gangway and drop their votes into a special pot. The senators did not approve, as it weakened their influence over the voters.

Senate wanted. Perhaps because the system was easily controlled in this way, the republican system proved stable enough to last far longer than the democracies of Greece.

Modern politicians still use political skills very similar to those of the Romans. When he was trying to get elected as a Consul in 63 BC, Cicero received this advice from his brother: 'You will need the gift of flattery. Though unpleasant at other times, it is indispensable [essential] in an election campaign. Your expression, appearance and language must be constantly changed and adapted to the feelings and concerns of everyone you meet.'

THE EMPIRE

Politics can be a dangerous, even bloody business, as many modern leaders have found to their cost. The greater their power, the greater is the risk of death at the hands of rivals or assassins.

From President J.F. Kennedy in the USA to Prime Minister Indira Gandhi in India, many modern leaders have been killed in office. Often their deaths are followed by periods of great tension, even war, such as that in Rwanda after the murder of President Juvémal Habyarimana in April, 1994.

► *Civil war in Rwanda, 1994. This savage conflict between the Hutu and Tutsi tribes left many thousands of people dead or homeless.*

The Romans knew all about such risks. Even the smooth-running republic could not survive the ambition and greed of its last leaders.

In 49 BC, Julius Caesar, the great general and conqueror of Gaul (modern France), marched his army south and seized the city of Rome. He was made Dictator for life, with complete control of the army, the treasury and the Senate. Though he refused to accept a crown, he became king in all but name. He wore purple robes and even put his portrait on coins – an act that was unthinkable in a republic.

The murder of Caesar in 44 BC began a bloodbath, as his successors fought each other for power. For a time, the Consul Mark Antony seemed to be gaining control, thanks to the support of the army in Italy. But Brutus and Cassius, Caesar's murderers, had powerful support from the army abroad and civil war broke out. Eventually in 31 BC, it was Caesar's nephew Octavian who successfully defeated all his rivals to become sole ruler. As so often since, political arguments were settled by military might.

The Senate gave Octavian the title 'Augustus', meaning 'highly thought of', and he became the first emperor of the Roman world. Once in power, Augustus ruled wisely. He believed that even the emperor was not above the law. He unified the empire and gave Rome a police force, a fire brigade, clean water and ample supplies of corn.

Caesar's ambition
When Julius Caesar marched through a small village, he said, 'I would rather be the first man here than the second man in Rome itself.' No wonder the Roman senators feared him!

▼ *A nineteenth-century illustration of the murder of Julius Caesar, in 44 BC. Caesar's death led to the downfall of the republican system and its replacement by an empire.*

▲ *Roman emperors such as Julius Caesar used coins as political messages. His portrait told everyone who was in charge. In 1991, a new government came to power in Russia. It reissued all the country's banknotes to show the new Russian flag in place of the old Communist hammer-and-sickle sign.*

Twentieth-century dictators such as Adolf Hitler and Saddam Hussein have usually had evil reputations. This was certainly deserved by some Roman emperors too.

Emperor Caligula (AD 37–41) was mentally ill. People feared him for his terrible cruelty but despised him for such acts as threatening to make his horse, Incitatus, a Consul. His successor Claudius (AD 41–54) was poisoned by his wife so that her own son Nero (AD 54–68) could be emperor. He repaid his mother by murdering her, his wife and brother-in-law, and is best known for throwing Christians to the lions and burning down the city of Rome. The later Emperor Domitian (AD 81–96) simply executed anyone who disagreed with him.

When wisely used, the emperor's authority brought peace, prosperity and justice to the whole empire. The idea of natural law – that all citizens are born with certain rights – was a Roman invention. To the Romans, in theory at least, it offered most people fair treatment. Unlike the Greeks, the Romans let all who lived in the empire, apart from slaves, become citizens, whatever their race. During the

nineteenth century, Britain was to copy this idea. Some modern countries, like Australia, have gone back to the Greek model and have strict conditions of citizenship.

Perhaps the Romans' greatest political achievement was in managing to rule such a vast empire at all. All modern governments need efficient communications. The Romans first developed these through a network of roads and bridges, some of which are still used today. News, the post, traders, and above all, soldiers, could speedily reach every corner of the empire.

But eventually, even this system began to break down. The strains of controlling and protecting so many different provinces and such long borders began to show. By the early 300s, the empire was frequently split between east and west, with separate capitals at Constantinople (modern Istanbul) and Rome. During the fifth century, the Romans were constantly under attack from tribes from northern Europe. The Roman Empire crumbled, like all others before and since.

▼ *The Roman emperors relied on good communications and a powerful army to hold their empire together. Engineering achievements such as the Pont du Gard aqueduct near Nîmes in France brought prosperity to cities all over the empire.*

Social service
A modern proverb says, 'A hungry man is an angry man'. The Roman emperors realized this too and gave poor people in Rome free food and entertainments to keep them happy. Most governments today still provide some support for people in need in the form of a social service.

chapter six

ANCIENT
CHINA

Some countries today are cut off from the rest of the world. Even now, few westerners visit China. In ancient times too, Chinese people had almost no contact with the outside world. The people in the other civilizations in this book did not even know that China existed! China has the world's oldest living culture. Unlike the rest of the world, there is no clear division between ancient and modern times. Political ideas and systems of government from over 3,000 years ago continued until the Chinese Empire ended in 1911. In some respects, China's ancient legacy is alive even today.

▼ *The Great Wall was completed by Emperor Shi Huang-Di in 214 BC. It protected China from attack, but also helped to seal the country off from outside influences. In modern times, the Berlin Wall (recently removed) had a similar purpose.*

Chinese history is usually divided into a number of 'dynasties', or periods when one particular family was in control. It was during the Shang dynasty (1750–1050 BC) that Chinese writing first developed, along with an accurate calendar and a system of weights and measures. Then, as now, these were essential tools which enabled the rulers of northern China to control their people. As has so often happened since – for example in the former Yugoslavia – the authority of the rulers eventually weakened, and wars broke out between smaller states.

For centuries the country was divided. But when thirteen-year-old Cheng became king of Ch'in (from which the word China comes), he began to reunite the country. After twenty-five years of warfare, Cheng eventually brought all the smaller states under his control, and in 221 BC, he formed a Chinese Empire, making himself the First Emperor.

Cheng was anxious to stamp out people's memories of life before his empire. In 213 BC, he ordered books to be burnt 'to make the people ignorant . . . and prevent the past being used to discredit the present.' Only books on farming, medicine and telling the future were saved. The following year, scholars and teachers were imprisoned or executed. Over 2,000 years later, the Chinese Communist leader Chairman Mao did the same. During the 'Cultural Revolution' of the 1960s, he imprisoned educated people and burnt their books, hoping to prevent criticism of his government.

Like the Roman emperors, Cheng built roads to improve communications and assist army movements. His greatest surviving monument is the Great Wall, built to protect China against attack from the north.

Confucius
Confucius (551– 479 BC) was the greatest Chinese thinker. He taught 'Li', a system of good manners, honesty and obedience, which everyone was expected to follow. This code of behaviour is still a powerful influence in modern Chinese society.

Modern China is still the most populated country in the world. It seems incredible that such a vast land, with perhaps 5 million people in ancient times, could have been ruled by one man. Yet not only did a single emperor manage to rule the whole empire, but he exerted a rigid discipline over all his subjects. As today, Chinese people were probably more tightly controlled than anywhere else in the world.

What made this possible was the civil service, set up to serve the emperors during the Han Dynasty (206 BC–AD 210). This great army of government officials were the most respected people in China after the emperor himself. Civil services are just as important for modern governments today, organizing taxes and running other government affairs.

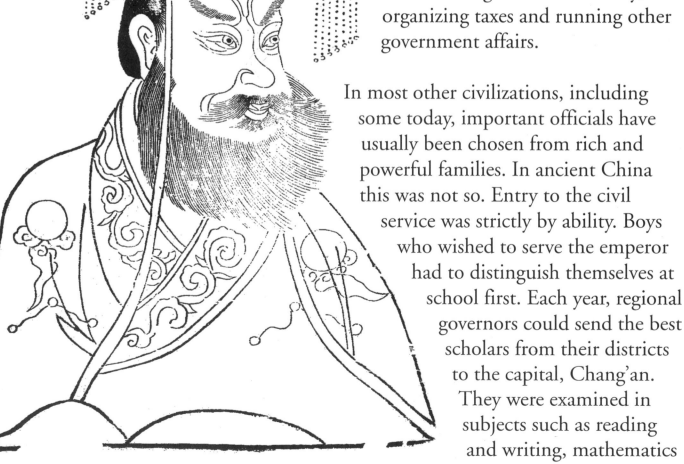

▼ *A seventeenth-century drawing of Shi Huang-Di, who became the First Emperor of all China in 221 BC. Wars broke out again on his death in 210 BC, but peace was restored in 206 BC, when Liu Bang became the first emperor of the Han dynasty.*

In most other civilizations, including some today, important officials have usually been chosen from rich and powerful families. In ancient China this was not so. Entry to the civil service was strictly by ability. Boys who wished to serve the emperor had to distinguish themselves at school first. Each year, regional governors could send the best scholars from their districts to the capital, Chang'an. They were examined in subjects such as reading and writing, mathematics

and poetry. If the scholars passed, they started government work at a junior level according to their marks (first, second or third class). If they did well, they could take more exams later to progress to the top jobs. Few modern states have created such equal opportunities for their civil servants – except perhaps China! It was not until 2,000 years later that the West adopted the same system of entry into the civil service – one based on ability.

In ancient China, civil servants continued to be tested after they had got the job. Every three years, the authorities had to send reports to the emperor about their junior officials. Each man's age, height and reading levels were recorded. Their abilities were graded 'high', 'medium' or 'low', and on this basis they might be promoted or demoted. Chinese officials were not allowed to work in their own home districts. This was to prevent cheating, or favouritism towards their families.

▲ *Throughout his life, Shi Huang-Di was troubled by fears about death, and life after death. These life-sized pottery soldiers were buried in pits to guard the entrance to his tomb.*

Badges of office
Ancient Chinese officials wore seal-shaped badges. These were graded into gold, silver or bronze with purple, blue, yellow or black ribbons according to their importance.

39

chapter seven

ANCIENT AMERICAS

Religious ceremonies
The ancient Mexicans devised elaborate ceremonies to keep their gods happy. One was a ritual team game played with a rubber ball. Others involved human sacrifice on the temple roofs. The king's control of these events gave him great power over his subjects.

Today, church and state are often still closely related. Many people see a political message in the teachings of Christ or Muhammad. Others use the powers of government to further their religious ends. The civilizations of ancient Meso (middle) and South America were the product of the most intense and fearful religious beliefs. This is reflected in the construction of huge temple-pyramids, many of which survive today.

A large number of such temples were built in the ancient city of Teotihuacan, in modern-day Mexico. Teotihuacan, was built in the first century BC, and grew to become the sixth-largest city in the world by AD 500. The great number of temples, including the Sun and Moon pyramids,

► *The Pyramid of the Magician, in Uxmal, Mexico. The temple on the top was used for sacrificing people to win the support of the gods.*

shows that the city must have been ruled on a strong religious basis. Teotihuacan had a population of about 250,000 people. Its streets were laid out in a grid pattern, and its people were divided into zones according to their jobs or their social status.

The cities of the Mayan civilization, which was at its peak about AD 250–900, were also dominated by vast temple complexes. Cities such as Tikal, in modern-day Belize, had temple complexes built, each with a pyramid of up to 70 metres high.

Mayan pictures, sculptures and writings constantly stress one thing – the relationships between their kings and the gods. Like the Egyptian pharaohs, Mayan kings acted as go-betweens between the people and the gods. In both civilizations, the kings were thought to control the seasonal arrival of water, which was necessary for farming. Whereas in Egypt, people believed that the pharaohs influenced the flooding of the Nile every year, Mayan kings were believed to control the annual rainy season. Also like the Egyptian pharaohs, Mayan kings became gods when they died. The Mayan kings passed their authority from father to son, and traced their descent directly back to the gods, whom they represented.

▲ An ancient Mayan priest sacrifices a man in a special religious ceremony.

chapter eight

ANCIENT
CELTS

Today, most people in the West are grouped according to their country or nationality. However, some people also belong to tribes. Tribes are smaller social groups than the population of most countries, and are ruled by their own leader. In Africa, Asia, North and South America, Papua New Guinea, Australia and New Zealand, there are often many tribes within a nation, such as those within the Yanomamo people of Brazil. The Celtic peoples of ancient Europe were divided into tribes, and would have lived according to their tribe's laws. From about 750 BC–AD 100, these tribes ruled much of Central Europe and parts of Spain, Greece and Asia.

▼ *A reconstructed Celtic round house. Tribesmen would gather in the chiefs' house to hear the druids recite their laws or sing of the great events of their history.*

◀ *Chief Raoni of the Kayapo nation in Brazil addresses the elders of his people, just as the chiefs of ancient Celtic tribes would have done over 2,000 years ago.*

The government of a Celtic tribe was in the hands of a chief or king, assisted by religious officials called druids. The druids were the most influential people in each tribe, apart from its chief. They were selected from the most intelligent young boys and trained for twenty years. During this time, they had to learn by heart all the laws and customs of the tribe. Once qualified, their job, like a modern politician's, was to advise the chief. They also acted as judges. As religious officials, they supervised ceremonies including (according to the Romans) human sacrifices. By 100 BC, some of the Celtic tribes in Gaul (modern-day France) were being ruled by an annually elected magistrate, called a 'vergobret'. However, the chief was still the Celts' most important leader.

Although the Celts exercised strong leadership, tribal customs made the people of the tribe firstly responsible towards each other rather than to a remote government. If one person harmed another, he or she paid their debt to the injured person's family, not to society as a whole. Even on the battlefield, people fought for themselves with no planned strategy – which made the Celts easily conquered by the disciplined Roman army.

Tribal justice
In 1994, six young Australian Aborigines were caught stealing cars in the Northern Territory of Australia. Instead of taking them to court, the police handed them over to their tribal elders, who punished them according to tribal custom. The same year in the USA, a Washington judge turned two young Alaskan Indians, of the Tlingit tribe, over to their tribal judge for punishment, rather than sending them to the Washington State prison. The Tlingit tribal court sentenced the two young men to banishment on separate, uninhabited islands for twelve to eighteen months as their punishment for attacking a pizza deliveryman and robbing him of $40.

Northern Europe

Before 3000 BC	2000 BC	1000 BC	0	AD

6000
First farmers in Europe.

2750
Stonehenge construction starts in England.

2000
Fortifed villages built in Eastern Europe.

1500
Stonehenge construction finished in England.

800
First Celtic societies begin in Germany.

500
Celtic lake villages are built in Austria.

390
Celts attack Northern Italy.

122
Hadrian's wall is built in Britain.

410
Visigoths sack Rome.

440
Angles and Saxons settle in Britain.

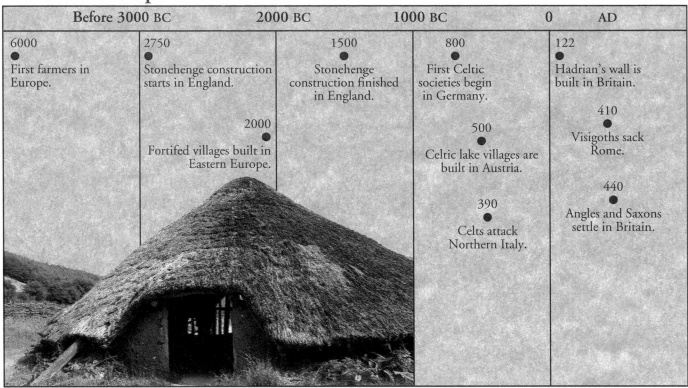

The Mediterranean Lands

Before 3000 BC	2000 BC	1000 BC	0	AD

3000
Bronze Age people in Crete.

2500
Minoan culture begins in Crete, then spreads to other Mediterranean lands.

1800–1450
Peak of Minoan civilization in Crete.

1450–1100
Peak of Mycenean civilization in Greece.

1200
Greeks destroy Troy in Turkey.

1000
Etruscan civilization in Italy.

700
City of Rome founded.

594
Solon reforms the laws of Athens.

505
Democracy begins in Athens.

336 – 323
Alexander the Great rules the Macedonian Empire.

44
Julius Caesar is murdered.

14
Death of Augustus, first Roman Emperor.

33
Death of Jesus Christ in Jerusalem.

337
Roman Empire becomes Christian under Constantine.

476
End of the Roman Empire in the West.

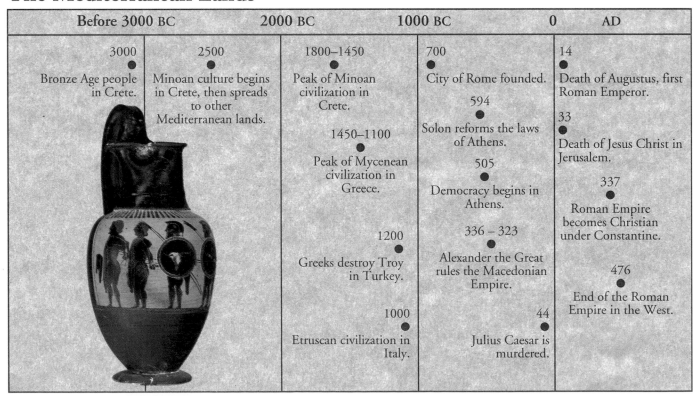

The Far East and Americas

Before 3000 BC	2000 BC	1000 BC	0 AD	
6000 First farmers in China. **4000** First towns in India. **3000** First farmers in North America. First villages in Mexico.	**2500** Towns started in Peru, South America.	**1760-1050** Shang dynasty in China. **1500** Early city states in India. **1200–400** Peak of Olmec civilization in Mexico.	**480** Death of Confucius. **221** Cheng becomes the First Emperor of the whole of China. Great Wall built.	**250–900** Peak of Mayan civilization in Mexico. **300** City of Teotihuacan in Mexico has 200,000 people. **530** Mayan city of Chichen Itza built in Mexico.

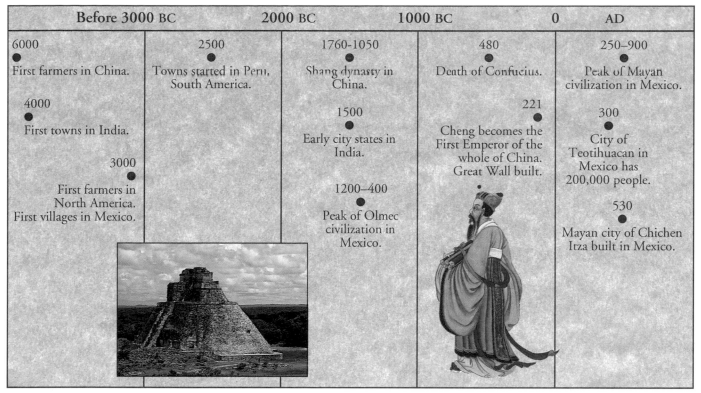

The Middle East and Egypt

Before 3000 BC	2000 BC	1000 BC	0 AD	
9000 The first known city, Jericho, is built. **6200** The city of Çatal Hüyük is built in Turkey. **3500** First city states in Mesopotamia. **3300** Writing begins in Mesopotamia. **3100** Egypt is united under the first pharaohs.	**3000** First bronze tools used in the Middle East. **2600** Egyptian pharaohs build pyramids at Giza, Egypt. **2200** City of Ur flourishes in Mesopotamia.	**1792–1750** Hammurabi is King of Babylon. **1650–1200** Hittite Empire. **1500** Queen Hatshepsut rules Egypt.	**945** Civil war in Egypt splits the country into small states. **606** Babylonians conquer Egypt. **332** Alexander the Great conquers Egypt. **30** Egypt becomes part of the Roman Empire.	**116** Roman Empire extends into Persia. **571** Prophet Muhammad born in Mecca, Arabia.

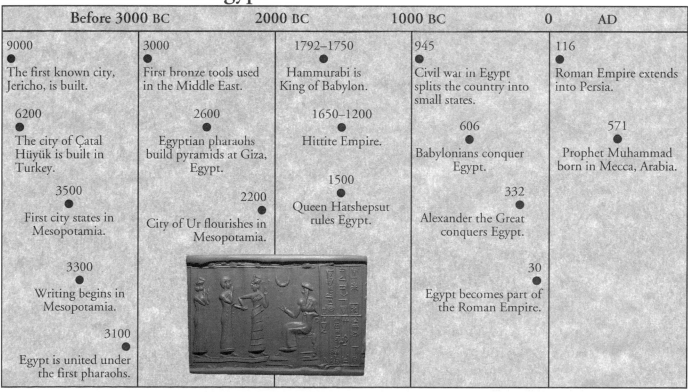

45

GLOSSARY

Aborigines   The original inhabitants of Australia.

Abundant   Plentiful.

Administrators   People who carry out government business.

Assassinated   Murdered for political reasons.

Census   An official counting of the population of a country.

Citizens   Members of a state, who are subject to its government and laws.

Civil service   The various branches of a government apart from the army.

Communications   Methods of sending information, including roads.

Compromise   To settle a disagreement where both sides give in a little.

Debates   Formal discussions.

Democracy   A form of government whose members have been freely elected as their representatives by the people.

Druids   Priests of the Celtic religion.

Dynasty   A family of kings or rulers.

Economically powerful   Strong because of wealth.

Elders   Older, experienced people.

Emperors   Leaders of empires.

Favouritism   Unfair preference in favour of one person, even though others have an equal claim.

Government   A group of people who run a country – govern means run or rule.

Hereditary   Inherited from ancestors.

Irrigating   Watering land.

Magistrate   An important official of government or law.

Mass media   Newspapers, radio and television, which give information.

Merchants   Businesspeople who buy and sell goods.

Military power   Power from the army of a country.

Oath   Promise.

Ostracism   The exclusion of a person from society or a social group.

Policy-making   Making decisions about government actions, which are agreed by a number of people.

Social service   A service run by the government of a country to help people in need.

Strike   To stop work because of complaints by workers against the people they work for.

Treasury   A government department which looks after money.

Utterances   Words or spoken sayings.

Widow   The wife of someone who has died.

Viziers   The chief officials of the Egyptian pharaohs.

BOOKS TO READ

History Makers: Ancient Greeks by Clare Chandler (Wayland, 1994)
History Makers of the Roman Empire by P. Scott and A. S. Williams (Wayland, 1995)
Look into the Past: The Egyptians by Roger Coote (Wayland, 1993)
Look into the Past: The Greeks by A. Susan Williams (Wayland 1993)
Rome and the Ancient World by M. Corbishley (Simon and Schuster, 1993)
The Atlas of Ancient Worlds by Dr Anne Millard (Dorling Kindersley, 1994)
The Atlas of the Ancient World by Margaret Oliphant (Ebury Press, 1992)
The Earliest Civilizations by Margaret Oliphant (Simon and Schuster, 1991)
The Oxford Children's Ancient History by R. Burrell (Oxford University Press, 1994)
Timelines of the Ancient World by Chris Scarre (Dorling Kindersley, 1993)
Timelink – Ancient World by M. Corbishley (Hamlyn, 1992)

Picture acknowledgements:
The publishers would like to thank the following for allowing their pictures to be used in this book:
AKG London *Cover* (main), Title Page (main), 6-7 (bottom), 15, 17 (top), 23, 26, 30. 41 (top), 44 (bottom); Ancient Art & Architecture Collection 24; Bridgeman Art Library (Museo e Gallerie Nazionali di Capodimonte, Naples) 33, (17th Century Bibliotheque Nationale, Paris) 37 (top); Sue Cunningham 43; C M Dixon 11 (top), 12 (bottom), 27, 29 (top), 45 (bottom); Eye Ubiquitous *Cover* (inset), Title Page (inset), 7 (top), 21 (top), 31, 36-7 (bottom); Robert Harding 34 (top), 38; Michael Holford 13; Popperfoto 9; Tony Stone Worldwide 4 (top), 8, 16-7 (bottom), 28-9 (bottom), 34-5 (bottom); Topham Picture Source 5 (bottom), 10-11 (bottom), 12 (top), 19, 32, Wayland Picture Library 4 (bottom, middle, left), 5 (right), 14, 20-1 (bottom), 39, 40-1 (bottom), 45 (top); Werner Forman Archive 5 (top left), 42, 44 (top).

INDEX

Numbers in **bold** refer to illustrations.